SURRENDERING INTO SILENCE: QUAKER PRAYER CYCLES

DAVID JOHNSON

Inner Light Books
San Francisco, California
2020

Surrendering into Silence:
Quaker Prayer Cycles

Editor: Charles Martin
Copy editor: Kathy McKay
Layout and design: Matt Kelsey

Published by Inner Light Books
San Francisco, California
www.innerlightbooks.com
editor@innerlightbooks.com

Library of Congress Control Number: 2020933600

ISBN 978–1-7346300–0-8 (hardcover)
ISBN 978–1-7346300–1-5 (paperback)
ISBN 978–1-7346300–2-2 (eBook)

Contents

Figures

Gratitude

Gratitude to Trish Johnson, Marcelle Martin, and Elaine Emily for their help and spiritual support in bringing this work to fruition. Kathy McKay and Charles Martin much improved the manuscript as editors.

Preface

Quaker spirituality is one inheritor of ancient contemplative practices which are available in every major faith tradition, and it is based on the path taught and lived by Jesus, whose disciples were originally called the People of the Way. The traditional Quaker experience is that the Spirit of God communicates directly to each and every person, most easily when we spend time in silence, and is experienced mainly as an Inward Light in the conscience. Further, as this Inward Light is followed, we are granted more light and greater purity of heart or holiness, and we become reborn inwardly as the Spirit of God (Christ) takes hold of our lives.

Many of the quotations in this work are deliberately sourced from the first Quakers whose remarkable spiritual strength opened up a vision of true Christianity and changed the world around them. The language of the 1600s sounds foreign to our ears until it becomes familiar. Many words have had different meanings over the centuries, as is clear in the different wordings of the King James Version and Revised Standard Version translations of the Bible. I entreat readers to sit and feel for the underlying spiritual message of these written experiences of our Quaker ministers and elders.

This work is offered from the truth of my own experiences and in the hope it may be useful to others.

An Introduction to Quaker Prayer

Quaker prayer is a contemplative practice of surrendering into silence, seeking the presence of God that is hidden within our being. Contemplative prayer is universal and is outlined in the ancient Hebrew and Hindu Scriptures and in early Christian writings. It is a deeper knowing, perhaps better described as an 'unknowing or loving'.[1] It is a mystical experience in the sense that a mystic is a person who has such experiences, whose life and religion are not based merely on accepted belief or ritual but on the mystery of firsthand knowledge of God's presence.[2]

One term for this type of prayer is 'prayer of silence' because it is our silence we offer to God so that we might better receive divine consolation and guidance. God's first language is silence, and in surrendering into silence, we consent to listen to God. It is in silence that our heart is softened and made receptive.

The traditional Quaker preparation or contemplative practice is called waiting worship, waiting attentively and receptively in silence for whatever God might impart, whether obvious or hidden.[3] It is both an individual and a corporate listening to God. It is a mystical path, based on the common experience of the Inward Light as guide and teacher and on the early Quaker experience that Christ is present within, waiting at the inward door of the heart to teach people individually in the present moment.[4]

Such prayer is an individual opening to God without the intermediary of a liturgy or a worldly priest. It is practising the Presence of God. It can be as simple as lifting up the heart in humble love for God.[5] It is available to all — religious and lay people, young and old, rich and poor, male and female, learned and unlearned. Teaching us how to pray has been the great gift of the Hindu, Buddhist, Benedictine Christian, Eastern Orthodox, and Islamic Sufi traditions.[6] Each tradition fits within a cultural and religious framework and teaches that prayer is a primary path to finding the Way, and each emphasises the importance of faithfully following one tradition rather than cherry-picking from several traditions to suit ourselves. The traditional Quaker path pursues solely the contemplative practice, disposing of all devised cultural practices and rituals, to attain a pure attentiveness to God.

We enter with commitment into our inner being, seeking that silence, free of thoughts and imaginations, into which God can communicate with us. One typical practice from the Christian tradition involves reading a verse from a sacred text or noticing something sacred in the world (*lectio*), entering into a repeated attentiveness (*meditatio*), and, if grace be willing, being gifted with a contemplative experience (*contemplatio*).[7]

The ancient practice of 'centring down' to avoid roaming thoughts involves focusing on the centreline of the body and mind. Be prepared to be led 'down', which can be felt in several ways. The first is often a sense of sinking down from the head to the heart or, as the Buddhists teach, focussing your breathing on the diaphragm, starting at the nostrils and then following the breath inwards and downwards. When you become aware of thoughts, return to attentiveness to the path of deep breathing. This is a movement from the head to the heart, from rational thinking to deeper levels of awareness.[8]

Further, I suggest that this communal contemplative practice was used by Jesus and the first disciples. Note Paul's advice on worship to the early Christians at Corinth:

> *What then shall we say, brothers and sisters? When*
> *you come together, each of you has a hymn, or a*

word of instruction, a revelation, a tongue or an interpretation. Everything must be done so that the church may be built up. (1 Corinthians 14:26–28 NIV)

The Quaker method and path, both in personal prayer and in communal worship, is to learn to pay attention to the Inward Light and to follow the Light.

The Quaker advice is inwardly to 'stand still in the Light'. This is initially difficult to understand, for the first Friends left no specific manual though many advices related to prayer are in their writings.[9] One specific advice, upon noticing thoughts, is to look at the Light that illuminates them. Lift the inner gaze towards that Light and its joy, not to the intrusive thoughts. The next advice is to 'mind the Light', that is, to pay attention to it, and the final advice is to 'love the light', welcoming its message since it is illuminating a matter to make us purer in heart.[10]

Contemplative practice is not undertaken to receive mystical experiences. We cannot see, of ourselves, the deep truth about ourselves; we cannot be both the seer and the one seen. The Light, separate from us yet implanted within us, can show us the reality of who we are and our spiritual condition. The Quaker spiritual experiment and experience is that contemplative practice, immersing ourselves in silence, is the way for us to learn and for God to work upon us. Extended silence restores our ability to hear inwardly and to see inwardly.

Jesus' healing of the blind and the lame typically had two stages: the initial physical healing and then the spiritual hearing and seeing that changed a person to begin to know and believe in Jesus. We can experience such inward teaching in Quaker prayer, for the extended silence provides the opportunity for us to receive the Inward Light and Word.

Daily practice is essential for significant development in the relationship with God, a committed practice sufficient to balance the worldly activity and external messaging we receive daily. Many traditions teach a continuing pattern of practising awareness and attentiveness during the day.

Inward experience of the Divine is the only authentic path to Truth. This path is accessible to all persons and is the standard by which all sayings and writings are to be judged. Contemplative practices are the way to Truth.

Reflections

For this commandment . . . is not hidden from thee, neither is it far off. It is not in heaven, that thou shouldest say, Who shall go up for us to heaven, and bring it unto us, that we may hear it, and do it? Neither is it beyond the sea, that thou shouldest say, Who shall go over the sea for us, and bring it unto us, that we may hear it, and do it? But the word is very nigh unto thee, in thy mouth, and in thy heart, that thou mayest do it. (Deuteronomy 30:11–14 KJV)

The kingdom of God cometh not with observation: Neither shall they say, Lo here! or, lo there! for, behold, the kingdom of God is within you. (Luke 17:20–21 KJV)

Hearken to that in your consciences, which raiseth up desires after righteousness. . . . If you be guided by it, you shall find a Teacher continually present; thou shalt need no man to teach thee, but it will be a Teacher unto thee, teaching and directing in righteousness, purity and holiness. And if thou art diligent, keeping thy mind within, with an ear open to the pure voice, thou shalt find it present with thee wheresoever thou art; in the fields, in thy bed, in markets, in company, when thy outward priest or teacher is absent (it may be in the ale house, or at his pleasures and delights, or far off), and will check thee and condemn thee for that which no outward eye can see, and will . . . purify thy heart and make it a fit Temple for purity to dwell in. (James Parnell, 1655, aged eighteen)[11]

The silence of a religious and spiritual worship is not a drowsy, unthinking state of mind, but a sequestering or withdrawing of it from all visible objects and vain imaginations into a fervent praying to or praising the invisible omnipresent God, in His light and love: His light gives wisdom and knowledge and His love gives power and strength to run the ways of His commandments with delight. But except all excesses of the body and all passions of the mind are avoided, through watchfulness, the soul doth not attain true silence. (John Bellers, 1718)[12]

Over the years many Friends have told me that they no longer need regular daily prayer. I don't want to suggest that I am a better man or that there is only one way but simply that this has not been my experience. . . . I could not face the next day without a time in which life is renewed. . . . The essence is regularity and time — time to reach down to the level where I can begin to see myself and my work straight, where that strength we call love can break through my anxiety and teach me how to respond instead of react, where I am not ruled by conscience but by Jesus the true man within; the level where I can accept my whole nature and forgive myself and others. . . . Prayer alone can reopen the road to the spirit, blocked repeatedly by busyness, self-importance, self-indulgence, self-pity, depression or despair. (Donald Court, 1970)[13]

Circles of Awareness

This essay draws upon the teachings of the Benedictine monk Thomas Keating (1923–2018), who encouraged the practice of centring prayer by religious and lay people alike.[14] The concepts are renamed and extended to fit a Quaker framework.

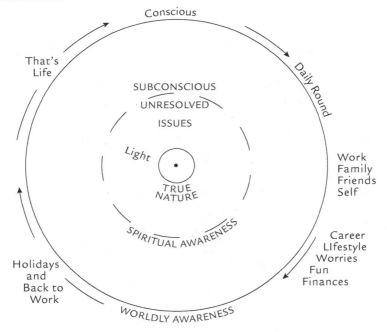

Figure 1. Representation of the circles of conscious worldly and spiritual awareness, and the circle of divine presence (our true nature) in the prayer cycle.

1. The **outer circle of worldly awareness** (see figure 1) is our daily round where our energies are focussed on the needs of our work, family, friends, and ourselves. Scheduling of activities, financial issues, meeting everyone's needs, busyness, watching out for our Self, and our own ego needs are all part of the level of worldly awareness. The whole range of living,

6

from physical and mental pressure to relaxation, is involved. Rational thinking, knowledge, organised planning, common sense, and cultural training are all in play. The daily round continues through work times and holiday times, year after year, for 'that's life'.

2. The **circle of spiritual awareness** lies deeper in our subconscious, a level at which we become far more aware of the divine presence within us and around us in all creation. We may remember times as children when this level was amazingly apparent and know that we have lost it during our growing up. We sense this level is a source of all goodness, love, and wisdom. There is a sense of spiritual potential which attracts us, even an awareness of the limitlessness of God. The distance between the outer level of worldly consciousness and the inner spiritual level is variable, but most of us learn that the difference is more significant than we thought. The level of spiritual awareness and the subconscious occasionally figures in some of our dreams and visions. This subconscious realm between the two circles contains much of our life history, experiences, and unresolved issues.

3. A **circle of divine presence** lies at the core of our being, what some call the **'true nature'** or the 'true self' or the 'Christ self', that is, the dwelling place within us of God's Presence, a pure wisdom, a source of universal goodness and truth and love and life and the divine Light. We may have only a dim awareness of this deeper part of ourselves that is peaceful, where there is no turbulence or anxiety or fear, a place which is an eternally reliable source of life and creativity. This is a place we may yearn to be. In that space, we experience divine union. Others might refer to it as the Christ Within, where our being is

totally '*hid with Christ in God*',[15] or as our Buddha nature, or as the Shekinah.

4. The **central dot** represents the divine centre and birth of our being.

This diagram is not meant to explain everything — it is simply a framework for summarising and understanding some of the mental and spiritual experiences common in the life of prayer. It emphasises the Quaker experience that the Light of the Spirit of God has been gifted to every person and lies within us and that Christ exists within us and is at work within us. This Light is first experienced as our conscience.

This does not mean the Spirit of God is only in humans, for this Spirit is present in all the created world, but this Spirit is within each of us and no person is devoid of it.

We do not cease existing in the outer world. Put simply, we can live on the outer circle, dominated by our worldly and self-centred needs and with no link to the spiritual depths of our being, or we can journey inwards and find that source of the divine being that enables us to live a life more centred in God.

Reflections

This effectual Operation of the Spirit . . . cannot be known without a being centred down into the same. (Elizabeth Bathurst, 1679)[16]

At the center of our being is a point of nothingness which is untouched by sin and by illusion, a point of pure truth, a point or spark which belongs entirely to God, which is never at our disposal, from which God disposes of our lives, which is inaccessible to the fantasies of our own mind or the brutalities of our own will. This little point of nothingness and of *absolute poverty* is the pure glory of God in us . . . like a pure diamond, blazing with the invisible light of heaven. It is in everybody. (Thomas Merton, 1968)[17]

A pamphlet from 1663, partly reproduced below, describes much of the Quaker spiritual experiences and understandings of the role of the Inward Light in guiding our journey towards God. It may take more than one reading to comprehend and may serve as a reference point for what is written in this essay.

The Light Upon The Candlestick
(extracts)

The Light (then we say) is a clear and distinct knowledge of truth in the understanding of every man, by which he is so convinced of the being and Quality of things, that he cannot doubt thereof.

From this definition which is here given of the Light, 'tis clear, that it must needs comprehend [include or encompass] in it the principal effect of shewing us, and giving us the knowledge of what's Truth and Falsehood, what's good and evil: which verily is a matter of so great concernment, that without it men must needs swerve up and down in continual darkness, opinion and sin, neither knowing truth at all, nor doing any good, but gropingly, by haphazard without any certainty.

This Light then, Christ the Truth, &c, is that which makes manifest and reproves sin in man, showing him how he has strayed from God, accuseth him of evil which he doth and hath committed: Yea, this is it which judgeth and condemeth him; Again,

This is the preaching to every Creature under Heaven, though they have never read or heard of the Scripture. This is it which leads man into truth, into the way to God, which excuseth him in well-doing, giving him peace in his conscience, yea, brings him into union with God, wherein all happiness and salvation doth consist. . . .

The Light is also the first Principle of Religion. For seeing there can be no true Religion without the knowledge of God, and no knowledge of God without this Light, Religion must necessarily have this Light for its first Principle. . . .

Without this Light, there is no power or ability at all in man to do any good. . . .

This Light is the inward ear by which alone, and by no other, the voice of God that is the Truth, can be heard.

. . . So that if the Truth of God be presented to a man who stands not in the Light of Truth, 'tis impossible he should understand it, although he hears and comprehends the words after his manner, yet he is still fenced off from its true sence and meaning thereof.

Hence, therefore, it is, that amongst so many hearers there are so few that have ears to hear.

He that hears Truth aright, that is, understands it well, must not stand out of, but in the Truth itself.

Therefore neither is it any wonder that all men do not understand and conceive those things that are brought forth by the Light. Those only that stand in it, are alone (and no other) capable thereof. . . .

. . . This Light, Christ, &c. is the truth and word of God. . . . For this is a living Word, and transmiteth man from death to life, is powerful, & enableth a man to bear witness of itself every where.

This is also the true rule according to which all our actions are to be squared.

This hath the pre-eminence before any Writing, Scripture, Doctrine, or anything else that we meet from without ['from without' means learning from outside ourselves, from reading or from another's words].[18]

Awakening and Beginning the Inward Journey

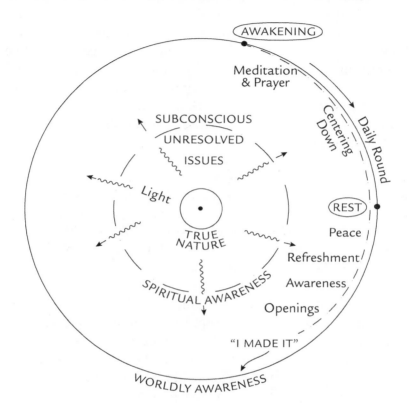

Figure 2. Representation of awakening and rest in the prayer cycle. A spiritual awakening is followed by desire for more knowing of God, which can be fostered by meditation and prayer. We can experience a 'centring down' (the dashed line), often to a place of inner stillness and rest. There, we may sense inner peace and refreshment and receive awareness and openings about our spiritual life. Our perceptions are illuminated not by external lights but by the Inward Light emanating from the divine centre within us. Not uncommonly our ego will respond with a comment like "I have made it!", which results in our awareness returning suddenly to the outer circle of worldly awareness. We begin our meditation and prayer again.

At some point in our lives, many of us are awakened by a mysterious presence of the spiritual life rising within us and feel invited to start a life of meditation and prayer (see figure 2). We become aware that we have a contemplative side to our being. We can be taught to explore this contemplative dimension in several ways — by practising awareness and attentiveness to our breath, by saying a mantra, by a constant inward invoking of the name of God, or, in the case of centring prayer, by taking up a short phrase or preferably a single word that arouses in us the awareness of God.

We may be drawn to learn meditation and practices of mindfulness, to participate in meditation or worship with others, and to commit to doing so every week or every day. These practices help us let go of our usual thought patterns and worries, our ego-centred thinking, and our dreamy imaginings. We learn to 'centre down'.

We are encouraged to accept daily disciplines of meditation and prayer, of reading the Scriptures or other sacred texts, of occupying ourselves by reading about the lives of others rather than watching movies or TV. We can become very enthused and fervent. We realise life is about something else. As we continue with contemplative practices, we find

- times of 'monkey mind' and torrents of thoughts or random memories
- times of progress
- openings of possibilities
- moments of calmness
- a steadier and slower heartbeat and breathing
- times of despair at being diverted without realising it
- the need to refocus our committed energy
- times dominated by expectations of ourselves
- the need to relax and let the process happen
- a sense of being enfolded or held by God
- a softening, a melting, or being turned onto a new path

Typically, this journey starts at a time when we are well immersed in our busy life. Our thinking is dominated by external happenings around us and to us, as well as our emotional reactions to those happenings. Rational thinking, focussed on family and financial and career issues, occupies us every day, and we value safety and security, power and control, esteem and affection. This is perfectly normal. There is little spare time for our spiritual lives.

We are invited into a voyage of discovery about ourselves and God. Beginning a spiritual exploration is a key point in our lives.

In prayer, we may readily find a place of rest and peacefulness or a sense of being enfolded, or of being opened up, or of being softened. Or, we may be made very aware of just how noisy we are inside! Many of us experience major resistances and hordes of buzzing thoughts or strange images, and we may need help to handle these. The ego or Self continually throws up alternative thoughts and reasons to divert our inward attentiveness. The alternation of grace and difficulty is as normal as night and day. Keep a little distance and notice what is happening. We may feel physical movements and changes in our body. Perseverance is required.

Whatever happens, it is a good start, for we are becoming aware of the reality of what is inside us. We may suddenly recognise the amount of time and energy this mental activity consumes and wonder why we had not noticed it before. Other insights and openings may happen. Prayer in silence has a mysterious, indeed miraculous, ability to heal and unify the divided self.[19]

Gradually, we become aware that we are not in charge of this process. We can put in the effort, though we cannot force the pace of the inward journey. This is different to our outward lives. We are not in control; God is in control. The ego is an impediment. The Spirit of God is working upon us, gifting us with various graces, both in our prayers and in our daily lives. We become more aware of God, and the more attentive we are, the more aware we become. We are being awakened to the possibilities of the spiritual life.

Reflections

[B]e no more than God hath made thee. Give over thine own willing, give over thy own running, give over thine own desiring to know or be anything and sink down to the seed which God sows in the heart, and let that grow in thee and be in thee and breathe in thee and act in thee; and thou shalt find by sweet experience that the Lord knows that and loves and owns that, and will lead it to the inheritance of Life, which is its portion. (Isaac Penington, 1661)[20]

[S]ink down into that measure of life that ye have received, and go not out with your in-looking at what is contrary to you, for if you do you will miss of the power that should destroy it, for as ye keep in that which is pure, which is the eternal word of the Lord, which is nigh in your hearts, it will work and operate so, that it will overcome what is contrary. (Sarah Jones, 1650)[21]

Now the only way to dislodge them, and to be rid of their company, is to show them no countenance, make no provision for them, give them no entertainment, but by the light of God, which discovers them to be your enemies, judge them, and keep your mind exercised in the light and Power of God, that it is turned to; and in your thoughts and imaginations, give them no regard: and though they do and may arise, pursue and compass you about like bees, yet you, keeping your eye fixed in the light and Power of God, which is as near to you as your thoughts are, and shows them unto you, you wilt see them, in due time scattered as chaff before a fierce wind, and destroyed as stubble before a devouring fire. (William Shewen, 1683)[22]

Now this is the light which you are lighted withal, which shows you when you do wrong . . . and you know with that when you have wronged anyone, and broken promise, and told a thing that is not so, there is something riseth in you that is a witness against you, and that is the light. (George Fox, 1656)[23]

Rest and Refreshment

Following the committed practice of meditation and prayer, we begin to experience times of peace and, to use the Quaker term, 'refreshment' (see figure 2). A sense of inner calm arises, a sense of coming home, of quiet joy, of knowing or being enfolded in God's presence, of a deep peace appearing, perhaps not for long but so helpful we yearn for more. The traditional word for this is 'rest', and the Hebrew word is *shabbat*. Inner peace and refreshment are not emotional states we can manufacture of ourselves; they are gifts from God (Acts 3:19). It is a peace the world cannot give.

Commonly, we are made aware of the depths of our being, of who we really are, and of the deeper possibilities of life. We may experience some deep understandings or, as some call them, 'openings' into our spiritual being or feel ourselves being melted and changed.

We can also come to feel 'I've made it', 'I know how to do it', or other temporary and misguided self-commentaries that start with 'I'. When this happens, the sense of God's presence inevitably disappears. The ego has reared its head. Thankfully, we know what to do. As we become aware of these feelings, we can regard them as just thoughts which are to be let go, and then we return to our breath or sacred word.

God favours us with sweet experiences, with showers of love and the opening of our vision into the spiritual world. Yet the main work is yet to be done. This is the start, not the end; it is the opening of a door, and we are invited to pass through it and start the deeper journey.

It may come as a shock to realise we are not really in charge of this journey — God is. This is very different from our worldly roles where we are continually making the decisions of what to do or not do or are giving instructions. In the spiritual life, we are the learners and servants.

Nobody knows why some paths are faster and why some take longer. The changes are gradual but great. Our experience is that, with practice over some months, our periods of deep rest become longer, and we are enabled to see thoughts for what they are and not be diverted so easily nor for so long. We begin to descend into the subconscious.

Sooner or later, feelings of physical discomfort may arise, a sign that we are being 'worked on' and that we have much more to learn. These times may also contain intimations of our 'unwellness', that we are not quite as good as we thought, not as wholesome inwardly, as we had imagined ourselves.

This deepening awareness is real progress, but we are not to take credit for it ourselves. The Light has started to show us our spiritual condition, the reality of who we are and of our relationship with God. It is important to maintain our practice and our commitment to the journey.

We become aware of those parts of ourselves which are blocks in our relationship with God. At first, it is tempting to reject these insights and rationalise them away because of what someone else has done or for whatever other reason suits us. This is a mistake. The Light has shown us these imperfections for the good reason that they need to be dealt with if our heart is to be purified and we are to grow in love and truth. In George Fox's language, we are to both 'mind the Light' — that is, pay good attention to it — and to 'love the Light', for it is showing us what God requires us to work on. In this way, we make steps to becoming closer to God.

We have the choice whether to accept and follow what the Light shows us or to reject the Light; that is our free will. God did not create us as robots. We are given the free will to say yes to what the Spirit of God is asking of us.

Reflections

Stand at the crossroads and look. Ask about the ancient paths. Ask what the good way is, and walk that way. Then you will find peace in yourselves. (Jeremiah 6:16 TIB)

"Come to me, all you who are weary and burdened, and I will give you rest. Take my yoke upon you and learn from me, for I am gentle and humble in heart, and you will find rest for your souls. For my yoke is easy and my burden is light." (Matthew 11:28–30 NIV)

Oh, the deep distress and sore anguish of soul I now feel! It is beyond expression; yet out of the depth of my tribulation have I been permitted this morning to cry unto the depth of His mercies, whose compassions fail not. Oh! There is something in me which perhaps is not of His pure Spirit. (Sarah Lynes Grubb, 1791)[24]

True silence is the rest of the mind, and is to the spirit what sleep is to the body, nourishment and refreshment. (William Penn, 1682)[25]

Whenever, therefore, ye come to feel this refreshing dew upon your souls, then take heed and wait singly in the sense of it, keep your eye to the joy that is now set before you in Christ Jesus, the Seed; for if you let your minds wander, there are objects on every hand to lead you from your soul's beloved. (Stephen Crisp, 1668)[26]

Risings or Eruptions from the Subconscious

The next stage of the journey is about to begin, and for some it happens very quickly. Our subconscious vulnerabilities and addictions are places we can be tempted into error.

The subconscious holds many unresolved matters, dating back to anxieties from our childhood or the confusions of identity and sexual tensions during adolescence, mistakes or dramas in early adulthood, failed relationships, harsh words, missed opportunities in our careers, or unhelpful cultural training. It may be grief over the death of a parent, sibling, or close friend, grief which we were never allowed the time to deal with because the busyness of life hurried us onward. It may be resentment and anger at how we were treated or opportunities we were denied.

Many, many times these events were left unresolved due to our lack of time to sort through the emotional debris.

The longer and deeper the periods of rest in contemplative prayer, the sooner and the more certain these unresolved issues will arise from our subconscious and interrupt our prayers or even erupt during normal life (see figure 3). The relaxing of our psychological defences allows unexpected images, memories, and commentary to rise into our consciousness. We learn to notice these but not be derailed by them.

Strong emotions from traumas can suddenly erupt and be in our mouths before we can stop them. We may find ourselves suddenly angry and answering people with inordinate aggression, or full of bombastic pride, or miserably unhappy and weeping, or full of fear and anxiety when facing even minor decisions. We may find ourselves unusually anxious, or angry, or depressed over matters which on the surface do not warrant such a reaction. We may project long-buried, unresolved feelings onto people or situations unrelated to the original cause of our emotions.

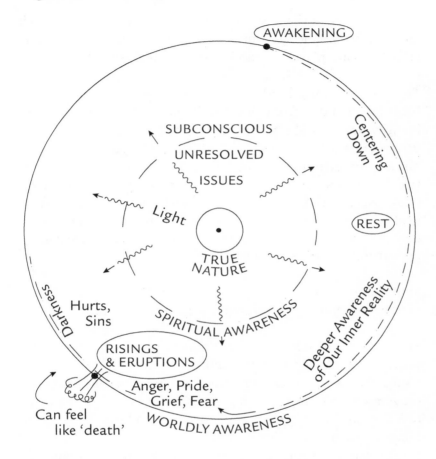

Figure 3. Representation of risings and eruptions in the prayer cycle, which inevitably appear as we enter a deeper prayer life. Some of these arise from past hurts or traumas. Some arise as the Light begins to show us past errors, what some call 'sins', and God invites us to accept the reality of these inner feelings, as part of healing them.

The stronger and more immediate the outbursts, the more likely they arise from events deep in our past, probably in childhood, even if a recent event has triggered or hooked up that emotion. The time has arrived to start dealing with these hidden, deeper 'corruptions'. We might say to ourselves, "Why am I suddenly so weepy or so hot and angry? That was over the top". An underlying, unresolved emotion has been projected onto a new event, and for some it can erupt very quickly and be in our mouths before our brain can understand what has happened. Our emotions have bypassed our normal self-control, and we behave quite out of order. Let us not forget the emotion of pride, which may convince us that 'we are in the right' and lead us to an inordinate and inflated sense of self-justification, self-preening, or self-promotion.

People experiencing eruptions of emotion can benefit from professional psychological help, especially if they are unwilling to delve into the spiritual life or if there are no skilled spiritual guides available in their faith community.

Thomas Keating labels this period of prayer the unloading of the subconscious.[27] As the usual busyness of the mind and the defences of the psyche and rational thinking are lessened, deeper issues begin to surface. Yet, this provides a wonderful opportunity for us to allow divine healing to start dealing with issues we have not been able to handle ourselves. George Fox talked about 'loving the Light' for it will lead us out of darkness and towards God; he also wrote of the Spirit of God acting as the divine physician.

If we resist these upsurges, we energise them and ensure they become more firmly entrenched. If we build a narrative around them, they become more established in our mind and we can find ourselves regularly trapped in a loop of unhelpful thinking. If we refuse to engage with them and push them down from our awareness, they fester and await the next opportunity to erupt. If we use alcohol or drugs, the same occurs.

Any disturbance we do not process or allow to be processed within us by the divine therapist, as Thomas Keating named that healing, will linger on. What we do not transform, we will transmit. George Fox called this behaviour putting off oneself onto others: "These said, it was they, they, they, that were the bad people; putting it off from themselves: but when some of these came, with the light and spirit of truth, to see into themselves, then they came to say, I, I, I, it is I myself."[28]

At first, the ego will justify our behaviour to us, though gradually or perhaps suddenly we become aware that we are way out of order, and we can feel real regret and shame. We recognise that these emotions rising are, as George Fox called them in his seventeenth-century language, 'corruptions'. God is inviting us to accept the reality of our inner being. Acceptance and forgiveness are paramount in resolving these disturbances.

For many people, these unresolved issues become more apparent in the later years of life. Is this because we have become less busy in retirement and have more time available, or because so many of us are finally drawn to prayer and introspection, or because God works more strongly in us to bring us towards wholeness before we pass from this earthly sphere? Some who work with the dying tell us that some people leave it till the last minutes of life to let down their guard and allow these issues to surface for healing.

Let us not view these disturbances as derailings or failures in our spiritual journey — they are essential steps. They are part of the spiritual journey towards God. Facing and dealing with these matters are essential steps. Welcome them!

How might we respond to such inner turbulence? One helpful contemporary Quaker practice is the Experiment with Light — a meditation based on early Quakers' discoveries that opens our heart to a receptive state, allowing the Light to illumine the risings from our subconscious and show us what to do.[29]

Reflections

[A]nd where the least degree or measure of this light or life of Christ within, is sincerely waited in, followed and obeyed, there is a blessed increase of light and grace known and felt. (George Whitehead et al., 1693)[30]

Stand still in that which is pure, after ye see yourselves; and then mercy comes in. After thou seest thy thoughts, and the temptations, do not think, but submit; and then power comes. Stand still in that which shows and discovers; and there doth strength immediately come. And stand still in the light, and submit to it, and the other will be hushed and gone; and then content comes. And when temptations and troubles appear, sink down in that which is pure, and all will be hushed, and fly away.

Your strength is to stand still, after ye see yourselves; whatsoever ye see yourselves addicted to, temptations, corruption, uncleanness, &c. then ye think ye shall never overcome. And earthly reason will tell you, what ye shall lose; hearken not to that, but stand still in the light that shows them to you, and then strength comes from the Lord, and help contrary to your expectation. Then ye grow up in peace, and no trouble shall move you. (George Fox, 1652)[31]

Do not stop to reason with flesh and blood, or dispute with the tempter, nor, as I have done, dwell over the temptation: for when I did, the more frequently, and with greater strength, were his assaults renewed. (Sophia Hume, 1758)[32]

When the answer comes welcome it. It may be painful, or difficult to believe with your normal conscious mind, but if it is the truth you will recognise it immediately and realise that it is something you need to know. Trust the light, Say yes to it. Submit to it. It will then begin to heal you. It will show you new possibilities for your life. It will show you the way through. So, however bad the news may seem at first, accept it and let its truth pervade your whole being. (Rex Ambler, 2008)[33]

Now, in this evening of life, I can look back over former days and remember the deep mental and spiritual baptisms I had to pass through to enable me to say, 'Thy will Oh! God, be done.' Lead me withersoever Thou wilt, and I will follow Thee, for it is a duty I owe Thee, and the salvation of my immortal soul depends upon obedience. (Rachel Hicks, 1875)[34]

Prolonged Darkness

There comes an awareness that part of our being, the more worldly, self-centred part, is clouding our vision of the deeper and more divine parts of ourselves, and this can be a troubling and painful exercise at first. My own experience involved a dark period that included self-loathing, which was not comfortable for me or my close family. I just had to go through this experience and suffer and then be led out of it. There was no viable alternative.

The Quaker understanding is that this darkness arises from our own resistances, our unwillingness to follow what God is asking of us. The spiritual advices of our elders are to resist any temptation to run away from these difficulties or to repress the problems because the process of accepting the reality of our inner being is a great gift. Unresolved emotions may arise from what others have done to hurt us, and these require healing. We are being invited into an opportunity to resolve our inner turmoil and to become more attentive to God's presence and work within us. If we continue in prayer, there is more chance we will resolve the turmoil and move closer to God.

The Light will also illuminate how we have acted from self-centredness, been hurtful to others, untruthful, in error, sinned, or done to others what we would not have done to ourselves. The Light shows us the sin, and we sense inwardly we have done wrong. We have not acted from a pure heart; in Fox's words, our "heart is not right before the Lord".[35] We are being shown where we have fallen from a right relationship with God. In traditional Quaker language, we have been 'convicted by the Light', convicted inwardly just as we might be convicted outwardly in a court of law.[36] We require reconciliation on our part with God, and we typically experience an inward motion to apologise or make reparation to the person we have harmed.

25

As we accept these motions, we find ourselves desiring to do what God is asking. Our own will is being step by step replaced with the will of the Spirit of God or what many name as Christ. The wonder is that God is ready to lead us into wholeness — that we do not have to carry the sin and be damned forever.

Having experienced some spiritual rest and then some spiritual upheaval, what do we do? Many give up at this point, saying, "This is not for me, I want something which makes me happy all the time". Yet, we have been guided and brought to this point for wonderful ends. One way to appreciate this darker time is to realise that God uses this time to purify us.

Three practices can help us handle troubling emotions and thoughts:

- **Welcome and Accept**. Learn to welcome and accept what is shown. Both the Experiment with Light and the Welcome Practice are helpful.[37] We tend to resist, repress, or shy away from revelations that we have serious anger, grief, pride, fear, or anxiety within us. If the Light reveals these deep-seated emotions or errors rising from the darkness, we do best to accept the truth that they are there. In this way, the emotions lose some of their grip and we can be shown how to handle them — not necessarily all in one go, though. Ask yourself, "What underlies this emotion?" or "Where does this come from?" or "What am I being asked to do?"

- **Let Go**. Becoming aware of thoughts and emotions, we let go of them as soon as possible. Some can be tenacious and require repeated effort, returning to our breathing, repeating our sacred word or mantra. The author of *The Cloud of Unknowing* advised us to let thoughts drop off into the cloud of forgetting.[38] Pushing

26

against thoughts only energises them. A Quaker advice is to not entertain the thoughts.

- **Lift the Heart and Gaze towards God**. When the opportunity arises, turn your inward eyes past or over these disturbances, looking to the Light which shows them to you, for that is the pure Light. We may imagine it as lifting our gaze towards God, the source of all our being and goodness and strength and love. We may pray for the opportunity to love God.

This inward suffering is a real and essential part of the spiritual journey, experienced by most serious seekers, and it is important to accept what is happening and not to regard such difficulties as abandonment or evidence of our own evil nature. We are basically, at our core, pure, and God is striving within us to bring this purity into our whole being.

Despair is a common way that the ego defends itself, or, as others write, that the Enemy, Devil, or Satan tempts us away from God. The answer is to resign ourselves to what is happening, sit with it, and, as far as we are able, humbly direct our inward focus towards the mercies of God rather than be preoccupied with our own self-centred misery.

Unexpected and extended darkness may also be precipitated by major changes in life, especially when grief occurs due to bereavement, the loss of a job, chronic illness, facing death, or trauma and injury. Yet these occasions, difficult as they are, can also be the birthplace for new life. It is not uncommon for a new way of living to evolve, and this may lead to greater trust in God, a different career, a greater sense of being called as a servant, or a specific ministry.[39]

The darkness can be a time when a seed buried in the dark earth comes to germinate and grow in the light of day, providing many gifts for the benefit of the whole community.

Reflections

You who walk in the dark, who have no light,
trust in God's Name and rely on my God! (Isaiah
50:10 TIB)

And that which could not abide in the patience nor
endure the fire, in the Light I found to be the groans of
the flesh (that could not give up to the will of God),
which had veiled me, and could not be patient in all
trials, troubles and anguishes and perplexities, and
could not give up self to die by the Cross, the power of
God, that the living and quickened might follow him;
and that that which would cloud and veil from the
presence of Christ, that which the sword cuts down
and which must die, might not be kept alive. (George
Fox, 1647)[40]

I fasted much, walked abroad in solitary places many
days, and often took my Bible, and sat in hollow trees
and lonesome places till night came on; and frequently
in the night walked mournfully about by myself, for I
was a man of sorrows in the times of the first workings
of the Lord in me. (George Fox, 1647)[41]

[D]o not look at the temptations, confusions,
corruptions, but at the light which discovers them, that
makes them manifest; and with the same light you will
feel over them, to receive power to stand against them.
. . . For looking down at sin, and corruption, and
distraction, you are swallowed up in it; but looking at
the light which discovers them, you will see over them.
That will give victory; and you will find grace and
strength; and there is the first step of peace. (George
Fox, 1658)[42]

Art thou in Darkness? Mind it not, for if thou dost it will fill thee more, but stand still and act not, and wait in patience till Light arises out of Darkness to lead thee. (James Nayler, 1659)[43]

[A]bout three years after she had made her man beat Miles, it happened that as he was riding from Swarthmore, near Houlker-Hall, he [Miles Halhead] met with a person, who said to him, 'Friend, I have something to say unto you which hath lain upon me this long time. I am the man that, about three years ago, at the command of my mistress, did beat you very sore, for which I have been very much troubled, more than for anything I ever did in all my life: for truly, night and day it hath often been in my heart, that I did not well in beating an innocent man, that never did me any hurt or harm. I pray you forgive me, and desire the Lord forgive me, that I might be at peace and quiet in my mind.' To this Miles answered, 'Truly friend, from that time to this day, I never had anything in my heart against thee, nor thy mistress, but love; the Lord forgive you both; I desire that it may never be laid to your charge; for ye knew not what ye did.' Here Miles stopt, and so went his ways. (William Sewell, 1774)[44]

Others, who were light and wicked, reviled us. I had, as usual, some dear and tender friends among the brethren, who accompanied and stood by me in this great exercise. These partook of the insults offered — the people throwing at them: indeed somebody was unfeeling enough to bring hot melted lead and cast it at us; some of which was found on part of the clothing of one dear friend. I retired to my chamber at a friend's house after this bustle; and oh, the sweet tranquillity that filled my mind!" (Sarah Lynes Grubb, ca. 1800)[45]

Perseverance

Seek and ye shall find. When the hand is laid to the plough, keep going and allow the fallow ground to be ploughed so that the seeds of new life may have new light and water to help them grow. We are truly on the way. Pray for assistance and guidance. Welcome any insights and openings. Trust in God.

- Accept the reality of what is revealed
- If unseated, return to your position
- Keep breathing and trust in God
- Give thanks for whatever is revealed
- Let God run the show, not you
- Resolve to persevere

We are shown what we lack. We open ourselves to the prayers which God sows in the heart.

Gradually, we find small glimmerings of Light that show us what to do, and we realise parts of us have changed. We are becoming a new person. The scale of time this takes may be years, and it requires great faithfulness as well as help from guides, both people and written works. A secure faith community is a great blessing.

The first Quakers had the wonderful assurance that if they faithfully followed what the Spirit of God imparted to them — followed the Light of Christ within them through all the ups and downs, the mistakes and consolations — then this Spirit which had started them on the spiritual journey would also see them through to the end.

- So, we continue our practice of meditation
- We undertake the outward tasks to which we are inwardly invited
- We re-enter the cycle of meditation and prayer again
- We experience recommitment, despite any difficulties
- We understand that doing the practice is more important than any thoughts of 'getting there'

- We realize that intentionality trumps inability
- We are given a measure of faith

There are clear inward evidences of when we are in the Light. An inner peace and happiness, a clarity and certainty of mind regarding what to do, and the first fruits of patience, humility, forbearance, compassion, and lovingkindness all arise naturally. In contrast, if we feel a lack of inner peace; if we have no rest for the soul and experience the confusion of being tossed to and fro, of oscillating between 'doing this or that'; if we feel anxious or aggressive or have a sense of self-righteous judgement; or if we experience the pushiness of being inflated by our own agenda, then we are not in the Light. Despite our own inward urgings, it is best to wait till the Light makes clear what God is asking of us. Here, we exercise patience and trust.

We are led to continue this process of centring down and engaging in contemplative prayer again and again. Notice the pattern is not linear — it is circular. The Holy Spirit extends to each of us an invitation to this transformative process that has a sublime end result, beyond the normal therapeutic aim of making us a better and more fulfilled person.

Our inner lives may be compared to an onion. When one layer is resolved and removed, there is another underneath, and another, and another. Wonderful. Each time one is resolved, we move closer to our divine centre.

We begin to sense the possibility, and the hope, that we may be transformed and enabled to live a life

- of love freely flowing
- guided only by God
- free of old, painful habits and anxieties
- capable of remaining serene no matter what happens
- in which our divine gifts are creatively and abundantly available to all

Reflections

May the God of peace . . . furnish you with all that is good, so that you may do all that is pleasing to God. (Hebrews 13:20–21 TIB)

I am sure of this much: that God, who has begun this work in you, will carry it through to completion, right up to the day of Christ Jesus. (Philippians 1:6 TIB)

So go on, I beg you, with all speed. Look forward, not backward. See what you lack, not what you have already; for that is the quickest way of getting and keeping humility. Your whole life now must be one of longing, if you are to achieve perfection. And this longing must be in the depths of your will, put there by God, with your consent. (*Cloud of Unknowing*, late 1300s)[46]

It is not that I have reached it yet, or have already finished my course; but I am running the race in order to grab hold of the prize if possible, since Christ Jesus has grabbed hold of me. Sisters and brothers, I don't think of myself as having reached the finish line. I give no thought to what lies behind, but I push on to what is ahead. (Philippians 3:12–13 TIB)

Dear friends, go on in that which ye have begun; for I can bear witness for the Lord, that his love hath been abundantly shed abroad upon us, without respect of persons, because those that fear him, and work righteousness, are acceptable to him: and he makes his truth manifest among us, and causeth his peace and mercy to rest upon us. It is true, that Satan doth not rest to scatter this, and to sow doubts and unbelief in our hearts; but we keeping close to the Lord, are preserved from his snares; and happy is he who hath found a place where he is freed from tempests: but before this place can be found, there are many hidden rocks that may be struck on, not unknown to me. And therefore I have true compassion on those who are not well past them all yet; for shipwreck may easily be suffered on any of these. (Judith Zinspenning, 1664)[47]

And if they came to walk in this light, they might therein see Christ, to be the author of their faith, and the finisher thereof; their shepherd to feed them, their priest to teach them, their great prophet to open divine mysteries unto them, and to be always present with them. (George Fox, 1653)[48]

Down beneath the fluctuating changes of heavenly elation and hellish discouragement we can carry on a well-nigh continuous prayer life of *submission*, "Father, into thy hands I commend my Spirit." This internal prayer of submission of will we can carry in the very midst of our busiest days. There is a way of carrying on our mental life at two levels at once, but it only comes with practice. At one level of our mental life we can be talking with people, dealing with problems, carrying the burdens that our calling in time puts upon us. But beneath all this occupation with time we can be in prayerful relation with the Eternal Goodness, quietly, serenely, joyfully surrendering ourselves and all that we are to Him. (Thomas Kelly, ca. 1938)[49]

[He] who invokes with sincerity, persistence, fervour, and total faith in God becomes the possessor of an illuminated heart. Thanks to the *dhikr*, he is able to break away the crust that veils the light of the inner heart, which is luminous by its own nature. Once this Inner Light is unveiled, it shines forth throughout the whole being of man since the heart is the center of our being. (Seyyed Hossein Nasr, 2002)[50]

Becoming an Instrument

Feeling called to a task or experiencing an inward prompting or leading to do something is normal and is an essential step in the journey (see figure 4). We are not given wonderful mystical experiences just for our own pleasure. It is tempting to feel we now have the hang of the process and decline to do what is suggested. If we refuse, we will find less progress, for we are taking control of what is to be done. God is in control of this journey, and we do best to leave it in God's hands. *Into thine hand I commit my spirit* (Psalm 31:5 KJV) is not just a pious sentiment — it is a guiding rule for the committed spiritual life.

There is a big difference between the deep yearning and thirst for God which is implanted in us and, on the other hand, the desire to have what we want that, on closer inspection, borders on spiritual acquisitiveness on our own terms.

Many desire good experiences and consolations but do not want the effort that goes with them. We are called to walk the second mile. The ancient advice was to love God with all our heart, with all our mind, with all our soul, and with all our strength. The key words are 'love' and 'all'.

The spiritual fruits of such surrendering are virtues such as patience, kindness, gentleness, self-control, love, and joy. We can consciously practise them, but their deep emplacement is a gift. These gifts are not given for our personal benefit alone. They are given to be shared and are for the encouragement, sustaining, and building up of all those around us in our communities. The supply is infinite, and the only thing stopping these gifts is our own tendency to withhold something for our own benefit.

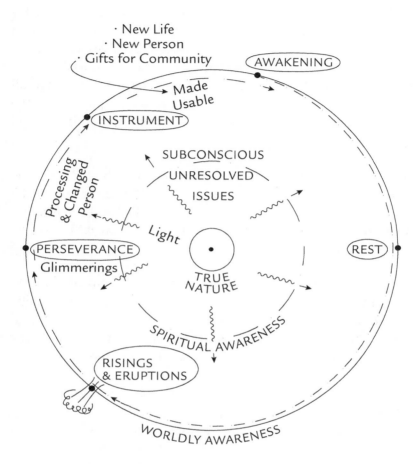

Figure 4. Representation of perseverance and becoming an instrument in the prayer cycle. In persevering through darkness and difficulties, and in accepting the realities of who we are and then accepting what is asked of us inwardly, we find ourselves changed and made usable. We become God's instrument. In continuing the prayer cycle, we find ourselves just a little more aware of the Light and operating in a slightly deeper spiritual place. The track of our (dashed line) path is now below the surface. We are becoming both more faithful and more spiritually centred.

Early Christians named these qualities as gifts intended for the building up or edifying of the 'body' — those around us who form the covenant community. Our lives only have meaning as we live to bring others into the Light, assisting all towards spiritual maturity. The extraordinary vision is that all will attain the full measure of Christ in a way parallel to the Buddhist commitment to live for the attaining of Buddhahood by all others.

Our reciprocal relationship with God requires we follow wherever we are led or prompted to go. We cannot learn the ways of God without following the paths lit for us. There are no absolute rules for what each of us is to do except be willing to become an instrument.

The primary Quaker testimony is to surrender our own will to what the Light shows — the early Quaker's drastic wording was to allow our own Self or ego to be crucified. That Light which shows us our errors and reproves us, if followed, has the life and power to lead us into healing and inner peace.

The other way of looking at this change is that we consent to God's presence and working within us, as Jesus explained about himself: *"I can of mine own self do nothing"* (John 5:30 KJV) and *"For I haven't spoken on my own; no, what I was to say — how I was to speak — was commanded by Abba God who sent me"* (John 12:49 TIB).[51] Our orientation is not about ourselves but about beginning to love God.

Gradually, we become changed; a new person is born within us, a being whose nature is to be more like Jesus. The traditional experience is of Christ being reborn within us and directing our lives. We do not have to feel anxious, for in accepting God's guidance as shown by the Inward Light, we are in very safe hands.

It is the Spirit of God, Christ, within us who is effecting these changes, for we cannot do them ourselves.

We come to live more faithfully as we are guided by the Spirit of God, which may involve

- adjusting our prayer life, perhaps reading and meditating on new texts
- doing our daily round of the 'small things' with more awareness and gratitude
- letting go of fear and offering ourselves more completely to God's service
- being more disciplined on a daily basis
- giving more to others
- laying down a commitment
- taking up a new ministry
- being open to being changed

Many have experienced the connection between a deepening prayer life and the clear leadings of God to enter into a ministry and work for the benefit of others. Living under the guidance of the Spirit means doing what we are guided to do. Any true and sustainable ministry arises out of a long and continuing prayer life. Holy obedience is required to lay down commitments or to take up new work, especially when this involves significant changes in life. Yet the evidence from many is that we are enabled to do so and are given the courage or strength or words we need. Our spiritual growth does not continue until we have heeded the call.

If we decline a prompting or leading, it is common that our spiritual journey stands still until we accede to God's guidance. The inward life is intimately linked to the outer work. No person is to put their lamp under the table (Matthew 5:15). We are to both hear and do.[52]

Reflections

The fruit of the Spirit is love, joy, peace, patient endurance, kindness, generosity, faithfulness, gentleness and self-control. . . . Those who belong to Christ Jesus have crucified their ego, with its passions and desires. So since we live by the Spirit, let us follow her lead. We must stop being conceited, contentious and envious. (Galatians 5:22–26 TIB)

And to some, the gift they were given is that they should be apostles; to some, prophets; to some, evangelists; to some, pastors and teachers. These gifts were given to equip fully the holy ones for the work of service, and to build up the body of Christ — until we all attain unity in our faith and in our knowledge of the Only Begotten of God, until we become mature, attaining to the whole measure of the fullness of Christ. (Ephesians 4:11–13 TIB)

Let no evil talk come out of your mouths, but only such as is good for edifying, as fits the occasion, that it may impart grace to those who hear. (Ephesians 4:29 RSV)

Practice hospitality ungrudgingly to one another. As each has received a gift, employ it for one another, as good stewards of God's varied grace. (1 Peter 4:9–10 RSV)

By looking at [Jesus] in the Gospel scenes we begin to catch glimpses of what God has called us to become before the world was, namely, other Christs. . . . [T]he field within which the treasure is hidden is our own life, and the treasure is our inner self, our Christ self. (Gerard Hughes, 1985)[53]

"A new heart also will I give you, and a new spirit will I put within you: and I will take away the stoney heart out of your flesh, and I will give you an heart of flesh." (Ezekiel 36:26 KJV)

Lord, make me an instrument of your peace:
where there is hatred, let me sow love;
where there is injury, pardon;
where there is doubt, faith;
where there is despair, hope;
where there is darkness, light;
where there is sadness, joy. ("Prayer of St Francis")[54]

[M]y desire is that all may be kept in the Lord's spirit faithful to God and man . . . in doing . . . to all men and women in all things that they have to do with or deal withal with them, that the Lord God may be glorified in their practising truth, holiness, godliness, and righteousness amongst them, in all their lives and conversations. (George Fox, 1653)[55]

Several years ago I had the experience of feeling called to go to speak in love and friendship to an old friend who had shunned me. I was very nervous. He might reject my friendship. I might make a fool of myself. But as I walked to his house, I felt that I was already carried by something bigger than myself. Afterwards I felt elated. I had answered the call. Clearly God had been with me, directing and supporting. (Patience Schenck, 1968)[56]

Companions

The spiritual journey has a curious dimension. We each travel our own path individually. Nobody else can do this for us, so there can be a sense of loneliness. We can have close friends, though none of them can know exactly what we are going through. Yet at one and the same moment of this aloneness we are also in the company of a host of spiritual travellers, whether they be in the same room, on the same retreat, or in the same dispersed community or are simply other seeking souls of any tradition. That is, at one and the same moment, we are both alone by ourselves and also immersed in a community of seeking souls.

God speaks to us through many spiritual companions, so we are to be open to the Light from wherever it comes. The Quaker experience is that Jesus' promise is fulfilled and thus we receive continuing revelations, anointings, graces, guidance, and wisdom from the Inward Light, Christ — or whatever term is most helpful for you. All we have to do is be receptive, moment by moment.[57]

God with us (Immanuel)

We can feel alone at times, even abandoned, while at other times we are well aware of the divine presence enfolding or undergirding us. While we are seeking God, God is seeking us. From ancient times, people learned they were not alone if they listened to God. The journey is not always an easy path, and God is not far from us if we lay aside our own desires and diligently keep our heart attentive to divine promptings.

Thomas Kelly observed that modern people imagine we are the initiators, but it is more true that God is the initiator who is reaching out and drawing us onwards, implanting divine desires in our hearts; in reality, we are the responders.[58] We are on a dual journey with God. The divine shepherd is always seeking the lost sheep. Many have experienced God as a co-worker, as opening the way, guiding and enabling them.

Previous travellers and their written works

The authors of many ancient through contemporary works accompany us. The Spirit which enabled those authors and gave them words is also our companion, encouraging and opening matters to our inward ears and eyes. The writers who faithfully recorded those words are our companions too. However, we resist becoming too acquisitive for knowledge; the journey is for our inner being, and our inward eye is towards the Light that guides us to God. The Bible is for many an inexhaustible source of spiritual companionship, as are many other holy books. So are the commentaries and written experiences of past spiritual travellers, many of whom followed their paths hundreds or thousands of years ago, and yet their experiences speak to us now and provide encouragement, hope, and wisdom. These men and women are our travelling companions.

Our living community

The other living members of our community are travelling with us, and this living community includes the entire created world — the stars, all living things, and the earth and grains of sand beneath our feet.

Gifted spiritual nurturers, accompaniers, friends, and guides cross our path.[59] Anyone in our family, faith community, or friendship circle may be the spiritual nurturer we need to help us on the path towards God and a truly centred life. All those called upon must themselves turn to God to become clear regarding what they are being asked to do. Their listening has two aspects: listening to both the surface and underlying issues in the other person and also listening to how God is asking them to respond, rather than responding from their own emotional state.

In traditional Quaker communities, the ministers, elders, and overseers accept responsibility for the spiritual nurture and welfare of individuals and of the community. The elders, primarily, as Sandra Cronk puts it, "were recognized as mature in the religious life and wise in the ways of the Lord. They helped people listen and respond to God. They knew much about the spiritual journey and could help others detect problems and find encouragement along the way."[60]

Spiritual nurturers can help in three ways:
- listening and encouraging the voicing of issues, then teasing out the issues with gentle questioning,
- helping their friend to clarify what is happening and to put matters in the perspective of their life-long journey, and
- providing guidance with sensitive offerings of specific, helpful advice.[61]

The Quaker experience and understanding are that God is always ready to guide and lead and goes before us, though we may be called upon to wait till we have been inwardly prepared. 'Way will open' in God's time rather than in our own time frame.

Reflections

And the Lord, he it is that doth go before thee; he will be with thee, he will not fail thee, neither forsake thee: fear not, neither be dismayed. (Deuteronomy 31:8 KJV)

But this is the covenant I will make with the house of Israel after those days, says YHWH: I will put my Law in their minds and on their hearts, I will be their God and they will be my people. No longer will they need to teach one another or remind one another to listen to YHWH. (Jeremiah 31:33–34 TIB)

I am with you always, even unto the end of the world!
(Matthew 28:20 TIB)

Therefore, since we are surrounded by so great a cloud of witnesses, let us lay aside every weight, and sin which clings so closely, and let us run with perseverance the race that is set before us. (Hebrews 12:1 RSV)

That as the grace and light in all is sufficient to save all, and of its own nature would save all; so it strives and wrestles with all in order to save them; he that resists its striving, is the cause of his own condemnation; he that resists it not, it becomes his salvation: for that in him that is saved, the working is of the grace and not of the man; and it is a passiveness rather than an act; though afterwards, as a man is wrought upon, there is a will raised in him, by which he becomes a co-worker with grace. (Robert Barclay, 1678)[62]

Now my dear children, this is for you to remember and keep by you, that you may always know the way to heaven's glory and to enjoy true peace and satisfaction. It is a straight and narrow way. Whoever thinks not, they are mistaken. Therefore, my dear children, keep unto the daily cross all of the days of your lives and to Truth's language [plain speech]. More especially, keep your heart with all diligence, for out of it are the issues of life. Then you will be brought nearer and nearer unto the Lord and grow in acquaintance with Him, which was what my soul yearned for in the days of my tender years, which I cannot forget, nor I hope ever shall, for I find the good effects of it from day to day. It bows my spirit and humbles my heart and keeps me in living remembrance of what the Lord has done for me. (Elizabeth Stirredge, 1692)[63]

Cycles and Deepening Awareness

The cycles of awakening, experiencing peace and rest, risings from the subconscious, perseverance, and becoming an instrument continue, with gradual increases in understanding and in life, power, and love (see figure 5). We come face to face with who we truly are. The image we like to project has some truth and also some falseness. Sooner or later, we will be brought face to face with what we may have dreaded — the realisation that we are defending ourselves in ways that cannot bear the scrutiny of the Inward Light.

This is not a bad thing. As we face these revelations from the darkness of our subconscious, we typically find they gradually begin to lose their grip on us. We may discover next time that an emotion such as fear does not affect us quite as strongly when the same memory resurfaces, or perhaps the fear is shown in another way for us to deal with. Later, we may find the fear does not recur as often or as strongly.

As we persevere in our meditations and prayers, going around the cycle, we find that God is gradually healing us. There is no certain end point. The layers of the onion continue to peel away. Yet, we can be given more confidence and trust. Gradually, we become more aware of the spiritual presence underpinning our lives.

A common result, and the time scale is in months and years, not hours and days, is that we become aware that we are not doing this alone and of ourselves. In truth, we can do nothing of ourselves. All is the working of Christ Within. As we become more aware, more attentive, and more accepting, God can do more with us. We become co-workers with God. Whereas we started on our worldly round allowing time for meditation and prayer, now the inward attentiveness is truly directing our work in the world. We travel on both levels simultaneously.

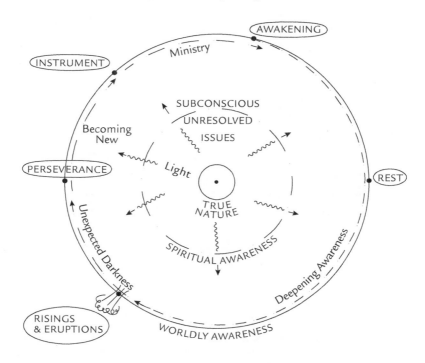

Figure 5. Representation of the complete prayer cycle. The outer circle of our worldly awareness and functioning is enhanced as we enter willingly the various experiences — diligently practising meditation and prayer, acknowledging the gifts of rest, and noticing the deepening awareness of the realities of our inward being. We learn to accept the periodic risings from the subconscious as opportunities for God to heal us and prepare us. Being willing to persevere is important in the transformation of our being so that we become truly useful instruments in a ministry operating under divine guidance.

Gradually, we are made more and more aware of the Light operating within us, and we find ourselves living on both the worldly and spiritual levels.

- We begin to find our inward journey, and sometimes our outward life, is moving in ways we had not imagined or planned. God is starting to direct us; we are no longer following our own personal, and often admittedly self-centred, desires.

• We become more aware of the divine around us in both the small things of life and in the big occasions. The Spirit of God becomes more real. We are part of the cosmic creation, of which we are a small part and are in no way entitled to dominate or exploit it unmercifully. We become more aware of the complete circle of spiritual awareness within us, not just periodic glimpses of isolated segments.

• We become aware of the cycles of darkness and aridity, even affliction, alternating with enlightenment and joy. We start to become more accepting of alternating experiences in the spiritual journey. The stages of awakening, and re-awakening, with times of rest are very pleasant. The analogy is being fed spiritual milk that is sweet and easy to digest. Then there are times of dry wilderness, risings from the subconscious or spiritual darkness, where we have to chew spiritual meat.[64] These are not absences from the journey; they are integral and essential stages to traverse, though rarely comfortable.

• Commonly, we may also become more acutely aware of pain and injustice and cruelty and greed around us. Sometimes this is pain we are just asked to carry as God's pain, and sometimes we are presented with opportunities to work against such malevolence.

• We become aware we have more spiritual and emotional stability. If we do lose our inward bearings, it takes recommitment, though not as long as before, to regain inward stillness. We become less reactive and respond from a deeper place. People may notice this change in us.

- The flame of love may ignite our heart, and more love, kindness, and compassion flow through us.

- We feel rising gratitude and awe and praise for God who has worked these changes within us.

- We come to know that our natural will and capacity alone cannot do what the grace of God, Christ working within us, can achieve — which is to initiate, sustain, and accomplish lasting inward change.[65]

- We learn to take up what God asks of us and to lay it down when we are clear our task is done.

The Quaker view is that when we allow our minds to run astray or place our practice and hopes in rituals, then darkness covers the Light and we feel God has abandoned us (Hosea 5:6); we have not kept our inward eye stayed upon God, who is available whenever we are attentive and who desires only our steadfast love (Hosea 6:6). The traditional Quaker understanding follows the experience of Paul, which is that the old person dies and a new person, who lives with the mind of Christ, is born within us. We become changed people.[66]

As we allow the Spirit of God to work within us, the fruit of the work of Christ as bishop is hope, and in Christ as shepherd we are endowed with gratitude. As we accept the teachings of the prophet, we find inner peace. In resigning our own wills and accepting the inward authority of Christ as Ruler and Guide, we are given the courage to do what we might formerly have been fearful of. In accepting the Christ as an inward priest, we find judgement transformed into compassion, and in accepting Christ as saviour, we gain the child-like qualities of humility and trust.[67]

Reflections

The Truth of the matter is, no one can enter God's kingdom without being born of water and the Spirit. What is born of flesh is flesh. What is born of Spirit is Spirit. (John 3:5–6 TIB)

"Oh, my weakness. . . . There seem so many mountains in my way and so many difficulties appear in my view that it appears too wonderful for me to go through". So it was indeed while I gave way to the Reasoner, which I have done many a time, my sorrow has been so great, that I have not known which way to turn. It has dimmed my sight, hurt my life and plunged my soul into sorrow, while I gave way to the reasoning pat. But it pleased the Lord to appear in the needful hour, turn back the Enemy of my soul's peace, and showed unto me that He would choose the weak and the dejected and them that were nothing in their own eyes and that could do nothing, no, not so much as utter a word, but what the Lord gives into their mouths. . . . Then did I freely give up to obey the requiring of the Lord with peace and comfort and received the blessed reward in my bosom. (Elizabeth Stirredge, 1692)[68]

We must be confident that there is still more 'life' to be 'lived' and yet more heights to be scaled. The tragedy of middle age is that, so often, men and women cease to press 'towards the goal of their high calling'. They cease learning, cease growing; they give up and resign from life. As wisdom dawns with age, we begin to measure our experiences not by what life gives to us, not by the things withheld from us, but by their power to help us to grow in spiritual wisdom. (Evelyn Sturge, 1949)[69]

The created things of this world are not free of ownership: "For they are yours, O Lord, who love the living" (*Wis* 11:26). This is the basis of our conviction that, as part of the universe, . . . all of us are linked by unseen bonds and together form a kind of universal family, a sublime communion which fills us with a sacred, affectionate and humble respect. Here I would reiterate that "God has joined us so closely to the world around us that we can feel the desertification of the soil almost as a physical ailment, and the extinction of a species as a painful disfigurement. (Pope Francis, 2015)[70]

A person who lives by meditation is never again alone, and neither is he ever again entirely a part of this world. If he is faithful in practising the Presence, within a few months he will find himself in the contemplative mood most of the time. Contemplating God and the invisible things of God, he become so one with It that there is no place where God leaves off and he begins. That which a person continuously dwells upon, that which he embraces in his consciousness, is that with which he ultimately becomes one. It is that continuous state of oneness which enabled the Master to say, "Thou seest me, thou seest the One who sent me, for I and my Father are one." (Joel Goldsmith, 1991)[71]

About a year before she died, she was sensible her departure drew nigh, for she found no engagement on her mind to travel abroad, as she frequently had done, when of ability, but said, 'She found her work was done and nothing in her way,' so was made quite easy and only waited for the salvation of God 'who', she said, in a reverent, thankful frame of mind, 'had been with her all her life long, and now I shall sing, sing, sing.' (Abigail Watson, 1753)[72]

Covenant Community

The covenant community is not based on agreed or idealised human rules and ethical stances; it is based on a communal acceptance that we are bound together by the thread of divine will. God has called us together, led us to together from all sorts of disparate backgrounds into a community of souls seeking to live lives obedient to the Light, lives under the guidance of the Spirit.[73] This is what early Christians experienced as the 'body of Christ', the allegory being that we each are members united in and essential to that body, just as physically our own bodies have eyes, and ears, and hands, and legs and all the other parts working as one; or, we are as living stones being assembled into a heavenly dwelling place of holiness.[74]

This places the responsibility on us to do the following:

- Allow God to teach each of us the deep spiritual lessons of living a life devoted to God, paying attention to (minding) the Inward Light, standing still inwardly when experiencing spiritual turbulence, and loving what the Light reveals. Maintaining a watchful frame takes effort. This Light is emplaced in every person to both show the way to God and to enable each of us to follow the way shown.

- Move from a life ruled by secular processes and norms, mainly modelled on the laws of an old covenant, to a life grounded in the new covenant of obedience to the Inward Light. It takes time to become aware of just how pervasive the old patterns are within us.

- Know beyond all reasoning that the foundation for each of us and for the community is not a set of rules; it is the solid ground of the Spirit of God, which we call Christ, which governs, reproves, orders, guides, leads, teaches, sanctifies, and heals our living together.

- Learn and teach the contemplative practices of meditation and prayer, which are the ancient pathways to God tested and found reliable by people of faith in many cultures. Only then can we each be changed into truly usable vessels for whatever ministry God intends for us.

- Notice, encourage, nurture, and anchor the variety of divine gifts entrusted to our community for these are the gifts given by God for the building up (edification) of our worship community, our broader Quaker community, and the whole world.[75] It is incumbent on us to help others become more usable instruments in God's service and to exercise these gifts with sincere humility and love and compassion and hope and courage.

- Affirm, praise God in gratitude, and delight in the rising and growing of the Light in each of us and amongst us and in the many ways we are continually blessed.

- Name damaging and unhelpful spirits and behaviours in others, initially with gentle guidance though with firmness if required. We are not here to accommodate all newcomers, and many may find our ways incompatible with their own desires or needs.

- Accept that we do not tell people what we know is best for them or us for we of ourselves can do nothing. Instead, we continually pray for guidance, and when we have come to know the Light, we convey sincerely and humbly and with deep love whatever message is given to us.

- Understand that other members of our community will also travel this cycle of prayer from awakening to the spiritual call, to becoming refreshed during retirement, to realising what is not righteous, to persevering through difficulty and darkness, to being transformed and healed into becoming valid instruments for God's purposes.

- Recognise that much of the culture around us will reject and ridicule and persecute our ways. Even many churches have accepted the tolerance, favour, protection, and support of the state and are well embedded in expedient systems and popular materialistic culture. The witness of God working through us does not seek their tolerance but instead challenges the culture just as God has reproved, challenged, and healed us.

Reflections

The life of this community is not sustained and upheld by perpetual ordinances and roles of succession. It is not a community that is started just once, in one place, and then expands from this one point. It is a community that comes into existence where faith exists and that withers and fades when faith languishes. . . . When faith ends this community ends. But Christ can create this community out of nothing. . . . First, as [the Spirit] is present in the midst of the *gathered* community, teaching, instructing, and guiding them. Second, [the Spirit] speaks to the individual member, and shows how to cultivate his or her gifts and offer them towards the harmonious functioning of the whole community. (Lewis Benson, 1968)[76]

I told him the Church was the pillar and ground of Truth, made up of living stones, living members, a spiritual household which Christ was the head of. (George Fox, 1648)[77]

This is the message we have heard from Jesus and declare to you: that God is light, and in God there is no darkness at all. If we say we have intimacy with God while still living in darkness, we are liars and do not live in truth. But if we live in the light, as God is in the light, we are one with each other. (1 John 1:5–7 TIB)

The individual whose commitment to the community is based on a sense that these community members are somehow special human beings, who have the right concerns and values and live the right lives, will have great difficulty when members of the community fail to live up to these standards and expectations. Being human we all fail repeatedly to live up to our own standards and expectations, we are bound to disappoint other people on occasion. If one's commitment to a community is a human commitment to the individuals in it, because they are the right people in some way, the community will be shattered when the individuals fail to live up to their ideals.

In contrast, the individual whose commitment is based on an acceptance of a covenant relationship says that we are given in relationship to each other precisely in order to help one another through these painful times, into a fuller relationship with God and one another. What is a centrifugal force in one case, is a bonding experience among a covenant people. Our individual sins and failures become opportunities for the community to practise true loving forgiveness, to offer spiritual counsel and guidance, and to offer spiritual and emotional healing. It is precisely the imperfect, human nature of the people in a covenant community that gives it the opportunity to witness the redeeming love of Christ, and the redeeming love we have for one another in Christ. (Lloyd Lee Wilson, 1996)[78]

Epilogue

The following summary of contemplative Christian spiritual teachings was drawn mainly from three Catholic quietists (Fénelon, Guyon, and Molinos) who had discovered a contemplative path to God similar to that of the early Quakers. The text was compiled by two Quakers and was originally published in 1813. It is included herein as a well-worded summary of the contemplative Christian spiritual path that is easier to read than many seventeenth-century Quaker texts.

[W]e make too little account of this internal Teacher, which is the soul of our soul, and by which we are able to form good thoughts and desires. God ceases not to reprove us for evil, and to influence us to that which is good; but the noise of the world without, and of our own passions within, deafen us, and hinder us from hearing him.

We must retire from all outward objects, and silence all the desires and wandering imaginations of the mind; that in this profound silence of the whole soul, we may hearken to the ineffable voice of the Divine Teacher. We must listen with an attentive ear; for it is a still, small voice. It is not indeed a voice uttered as when a man speaks to his friend; but it is a perception infused by the secret operations and influences of the Divine Spirit, insinuating to us obedience, patience, meekness, humility, and all the other Christian virtues, in a language perfectly intelligible to the attentive soul. But how seldom is it that the soul keeps itself silent enough for God to speak!

The murmurs of our vain desires and our self-love, disturb all the teachings of the Divine Spirit. Ought we then to be surprised, if so many persons, apparently devout, but too full of their own wisdom, and confidence in their own virtues, are not able to hear it; and that they look on this internal Word as the chimera of fanatics? Alas! what is it that they aim at with their vain reasoning? The external word, even of the Gospel, would be but an empty sound without this living and fruitful Word, in the interior, to interpret and open it to the understanding. . . .

Faith is an essential requisite for the proper performance of all our duties to the Supreme Being: indeed, without it we cannot possibly please him; neither should we ever be induced to seek him, or to believe in the influence of his Holy Spirit upon our souls. It is by faith that we are supported in our path to peace, and are enabled to persevere through the difficulties and besetments, which we may have to encounter on our way: it is through this holy principle that we suffer the pains of dryness, and want of consolation, without fainting; being thereby strengthened to "endure, as seeing him who is invisible." And it is only by faith that we can attain to the practice of true, inward, and spiritual prayer.

The prayer of inward silence is the easiest and most profitable path, because, with a simple view, or attention to God, the soul becomes like a humble supplicant before its Lord; or as a child that casts itself into the safe bosom of its mother. It is also the most secure, because it is abstracted from the operations of the imagination; which is often beguiled into extravagancies, and is easily bewildered and deceived; the soul being thereby deprived of its peace.[79]

Notes

1 Sandra Cronk, *Dark Night Journey: Inward Re-Patterning toward a Life Centered in God* (Wallingford, PA: Pendle Hill Publications, 1991), 57–62; John Main, *The Way of Unknowing* (London: Darton Longman & Todd, 1989).

2 Evelyn Underhill, *The Mystics of the Church* (Cambridge, England: James Clarke & Co., 1925), 9–10. See also the comparison of such revelations in Christianity, Buddhism, and Hinduism in Howard H. Brinton, *Light and Life in the Fourth Gospel*, Pendle Hill Pamphlet #179 (Wallingford, PA: Pendle Hill Publications, 1971). The traditional Quaker experience is of an immediate and continuing revelation unmediated by priests.

3 Lloyd Lee Wilson, *Essays on the Quaker Vision of Gospel Order* (Philadelphia: Quaker Press, 2007), 31–43. The teaching that waiting is a fruitful and essential practice is emphasised in the Hebrew Scriptures, e.g., Psalms 27:14, 37:34, 52:8–9, 130:5–6, and Isaiah 40:31.

4 George Fox, *Journal of George Fox*, ed. John L. Nickalls (London: London Yearly Meeting, 1975), 109.

5 Brother Lawrence, *The Practice of the Presence of God* (London: Mowbray, 1980); *The Cloud of Unknowing and Other Works,* trans. Clifton Wolters (Harmondsworth, Middlesex, England: Penguin, 1985).

6 *The Cloud of Unknowing*; Joel S. Goldsmith, *Practicing the Presence: The Inspirational Guide To Regaining Meaning and a Sense of Purpose in Your Life* (New York: Harper Collins, 1991); Basil Pennington, *Centering Prayer: Renewing an Ancient Christian Prayer Form* (Garden City, NY: Image Doubleday, 1980); Cynthia Bourgeault, *Centering Prayer and Inner Awakening* (Lanham, MD: Cowley Publications, 2004).

7 Thomas Merton, *Contemplative Prayer* (London: Darton Longman & Todd, 1973); *John Cassian: The Conferences*, trans. and annot. Boniface Ramsay, Ancient Christian Writers No. 57 (New York: Newman Press, 1997). See esp. the Ninth and Tenth Conferences with Abba Isaac.

8 David Johnson, *A Quaker Prayer Life* (San Francisco: Inner Light Books, 2013), 10–17.

9 Johnson, *A Quaker Prayer Life.*

10 George Fox, Letter to Lady Claypole [1658], in Fox, *Journal*, ed. Nickalls, 346–47. See also Stephen Crisp [1668], *A Plain Pathway Opened to the Simple Hearted* (Philadelphia: Benjamin & Thomas Skite; repr. Bradford, England: Henry Wardman, 1822), 129.

11 From James Parnell, *A Tryal of Faith* (London: Giles Calvert, 1655), reproduced in Charlotte Fell Smith, *James Parnell Died in Colchester Castle 4th May Aetat 18* (London: Headley Brothers, 1906), 81.

¹² John Bellers [1718], "An Epistle to the Quarterly-meeting of London and Middlesex," as quoted in W. C. Braithwaite, *The Second Period of Quakerism* (London: Macmillan and Co., 1919), 575.

¹³ Britain Yearly Meeting, *Quaker Faith & Practice* (London: Britain Yearly Meeting, 1999), #20.09. This quote is from a talk first printed as "Coping with Our Double Lives," *The Friend* 128 (1970): 1109–10.

¹⁴ Thomas Keating, *Intimacy with God* (New York: Crossroad, 2000), chaps. 7–8.

¹⁵ Colossians 3:3.

¹⁶ Elizabeth Bathurst [1679], "*An EPISTLE* To You five in particular, *viz.* A.W. E.T. M.J. B.P. & E.F. unto whom this is more especially to be Delivered," as quoted in Mary Garman, Judith Applegate, Margaret Benefiel, and Dortha Meredith, eds., *Hidden In Plain Sight: Quaker Women's Writings 1650–1700* (Wallingford, PA: Pendle Hill Publications, 1996), 403.

¹⁷ Thomas Merton, *Conjectures of a Guilty Bystander* (London: Burns & Oates, 1968), 142.

¹⁸ B.F. [1663], *The Light Upon The Candlestick* (London: Robert Wilson; reprinted as addenda in William Sewell, *The History of the Rise, Increase and Progress of the Christian People Called Quakers; with Several Remarkable Occurrences Intermixed*, 3rd ed., corrected (Burlington, NJ: Isaac Collins, 1774), 807–12. The original was published in Low Dutch in 1662 following the preaching of William Ames and was translated into English by B.F. in 1663. Republished by the Quaker Universalist Fellowship (undated).

¹⁹ Howard H. Brinton, *Quaker Journals: Varieties of Religious Experience among Friends* (Wallingford, PA: Pendle Hill Publications, 1972), chap. 5.

²⁰ Isaac Penington [1661], *Some directions to the panting soul*, Reproduced by Quaker History Press (http://www.qhpress.org/texts/penington/panting.html) and as quoted (without the first sentence) in Britain Yearly Meeting, *Quaker Faith and Practice*, #26.70.

²¹ Sarah Jones [1650], *This is Lights appearance in the Truth to all precious dear Lambs of the Life, Dark vanished, Light shines forth: Set forth*, as quoted in Garman et al., *Hidden In Plain Sight*, 35.

²² William Shewen [1683], *A Treatise Concerning Thoughts & Imaginations, in Counsel to the Christian-Traveller: Also Meditations and Experiences* (San Francisco: Inner Light Books, 2008), 95.

23 George Fox, *A voice of the Lord to the heathen* [1656], as quoted in Rex Ambler, ed. *Truth of the Heart: An Anthology of George Fox* (Philadelphia: Quaker Books, 2001), 28 (#69).

24 Sarah Grubb, *A Brief Account of the Life and religious labors of Sarah Grubb (formerly Sarah Lynes), A Minister of the Gospel in the Society of Friends* (Philadelphia: Tract Association of Friends, 1876), 4.

25 William Penn, *Advice of William Penn to His Children, Relating to Their Civil and Religious Conduct. Written 1682, first published 1761.* (Philadelphia: Franklin Roberts, 1881), chap. 2, #27. See also Matthew 11:28; Acts 3:19 RSV.

26 Crisp, *A Plain Pathway*, 129.

27 Thomas Keating, *Open Mind Open Heart. The Contemplative Dimension of the Gospel* (New York: Continuum, 1992), 93–107.

28 George Fox [1648], in *A journal or historical account of the life, travels, sufferings, Christian experiences, and labour of love in the work of the ministry, of that ancient, eminent, and faithful servant of Jesus Christ, George Fox* (Philadelphia: M.T.C. Gould, 1831; repub. on CD by State College, PA: The George Fox Fund, 1990), 87.

29 Rex Ambler, *Light to Live By* (London: Quaker Books, 2008). See the Experiment with Light website at www.experiment-with-light.org.uk/.

30 George Whitehead, Ambrose Rigg, William Fallowfield, James Parke, Charles Marshall, John Bowater, John Vaughton, and William Bingley, *The Christian doctrine, and society of the people called QUAKERS, cleared, &c.* [1693], in Sewell, *The History of the Rise, Increase and Progress of the Christian People Called Quakers,* 726.

31 George Fox, Epistle 10 [1652], "George Fox's Epistles," Earlham School of Religion, https://esr.earlham.edu/qbi/gfe/e001-020.htm.

32 Sophia Hume, Letter, January 24, 1758, in John Kendall, *Letters on Religious Subjects Written by Diverse Friends, Deceased*, vol. 1 (Philadelphia: Thomas Kite, 1831), 31.

33 Ambler, *Light to Live By*, 47.

34 Rachel Hicks, *Memoir of Rachel Hicks* (New York: G. P. Putnam's Sons. 1880), 257.

35 Fox [1653], in *Journal of George Fox*, ed. Nickalls, 156.

36 The seventeenth-century language of the King James Version of the Bible used the word 'convince', which meant in those times 'convict'. Compare the translation of John 8:46, which is given as *"Which of you convinceth me of*

sin?" in the King James Version and is translated as *"Which of you convicts me of sin?"* in the Revised Standard Version. For other examples, see Job 32:12 and Acts 18:28. See the discussion in David Johnson, *Jesus, Christ and Servant of God: Meditations on the Gospel According to John* (San Francisco: Inner Light Books, 2017), 87–90.

37 For more information, see the Experiment with Light website at http://www.experiment-with-light.org.uk/index.htm; 'Cynthia Bourgeault on The *Welcome Practice* and *Waking Up*', Wisdom Way of Knowing, April 4, 2017, YouTube video, 35:07, https://www.youtube.com/watch?v=_bClyhR2ZPc; Cynthia Bourgeault, *The Heart of Centering Prayer: Christian Nonduality in Theory and Practice* Boston: Shambhala Publications, 2016), 90–92.

38 *The Cloud of Unknowing and Other Works*, trans. Clifton Wolters (Middlesex, England: Penguin, 1985). See section 5, pp. 66–67.

39 Cronk, *Dark Night Journey*, esp. 97–122.

40 Fox [1647], *Journal*, ed. Nickalls, 14–15.

41 Fox [1647], *Journal*, ed. Nickalls, 9–10.

42 Fox, Letter to Lady Claypole, 1658, in Fox, *Journal*, ed. Nickalls, 346–48.

43 James Nayler [1659], *A collection of sundry books, epistles and papers*, lv–lvi, as quoted in Britain Yearly Meeting, *Quaker Faith and Practice*, #21.65.

44 Sewell, *The History of the Rise, Increase and Progress of the Christian People Called Quakers*, 82.

45 Grubb, *A Brief Account*, 15.

46 *The Cloud of Unknowing*, 60.

47 Judith Zinspenning, *An Epistle to Friends of Truth* [1664], in Sewell, *The History of the Rise, Increase and Progress of the Christian People*, 504–5.

48 Fox [1653], *Journal* (1831 ed.), 177. The scriptural reference to Christ as the author and finisher of our faith who is striving to bring us to perfection is to Hebrews 12:2: *Let us not lose sight of Jesus, who leads us in our faith and brings it to perfection* (TIB); *looking to Jesus the pioneer and perfecter of our faith* (RSV); *Looking unto Jesus the author and finisher of our faith* (KJV).

49 Thomas Kelly, *Have You Ever Seen a Miracle?*, in *The Eternal Promise*, 2nd ed. (Richmond, IN: Friends United Press, 1988), 143–61.

50 *Dikhr* is the constant invoking of the name of God. Seyyed Hossein Nasr, "The Heart of the Faithful Is the Throne of the All-Merciful," in *Paths to the Heart: Sufism and the Christian East*, ed. James S. Cutsinger (Bloomington, IN: World Wisdom, 2002), 43.

51 This holy obedience by Jesus is explored further in Johnson, *Jesus, Christ and Servant of God*, 2–5, 186–91.

52 See Deuteronomy 30:11–14.

53 Gerard Hughes, *God of Surprises* (London: Darton Longman & Todd, 1985), 113.

54 This is an anonymous prayer, probably written in 1912. See http://www.franciscan-archive.org/franciscana/peace.html. The prayer is commonly attributed to St Francis. See, for example, "Peace Prayer of Saint Francis," Loyola Press, https://www.loyolapress.com/our-catholic-faith/prayer/traditional-catholic-prayers/saints-prayers/peace-prayer-of-saint-francis.

55 Fox [1653], *Journal*, ed. Nickalls, 170.

56 Patience Schenk, *Courage and Spiritual Leadings, Friends Journal* (1968), as reprinted in Linda Hill Renfer, *Daily Readings from Quaker Writings Ancient and Modern* (Grants Pass, OR: Serenity Press, 1988), 139.

57 Continuing revelations were promised by Jesus in John 14:15–21.

58 Thomas Kelly, *A Testament of Devotion* (New York: Harper & Brothers, 1941), 29–30.

59 Trish Roberts, *More Than Equals: Spiritual Friendships*, Pendle Hill Pamphlet #345 (Wallingford, PA: Pendle Hill Publications, 1999).

60 Sandra L. Cronk, *Gospel Order. A Quaker Understanding of Faithful Church Community*, Pendle Hill Pamphlet #297 (Wallingford, PA: Pendle Hill Publications, 1991), 34.

61 Cronk, *Dark Night Journey*, chap. 8.

62 Robert Barclay [1678] as quoted in *Quaker Classics in Brief* (Wallingford, PA: Pendle Hill Publications, 1978), 62. This was also published as Eleanor Price Mather, *Barclay in Brief: An Abbreviation of Robert Barclay's Apology for the True Christian Divinity*, Pendle Hill Pamphlet #28 (Wallingford, PA: Pendle Hill Publications, 1942).

The experience of divine help in prayer whereby that God leads us and enables our journey towards the true peace and rest by working within us is attested in Philippians 2:13: *For it is God which worketh in you both to will and to do of his good pleasure* (KJV); Hebrews 13:20–21: *Now the God of peace . . . Make you perfect in every good work to do his will, working in you that which is wellpleasing in his sight* (KJV); and Ephesians 2:8: *For by grace are ye saved through faith; and that not of yourselves: it is the gift of God* (KJV). Ephesians 3:20 similarly emphasises this with the phrase *according to the power that worketh within us* (KJV). See also the work by Elizabeth Bathurst cited in note 16 above.

The French mystic Jeanne Guyon wrote a similar encouragement in *A Short and Easy Method of Prayer* [1853], *Wikipedia*, https://en.wikisource.org/wiki/ A_Short_and_Easy_Method of_Prayer:
> Though recollection is difficult in the beginning . . . the process is soon rendered easy; and this partly from the force of habit, and partly because God, whose one will towards his creatures is to communicate himself to them, imparts abundant grace, and an experimental enjoyment of his presence, which very much facilitate it. (p. 5)

63 Elizabeth Stirredge [1692], *Strength in Weakness Manifest*, introduction and notes by T. H. S. Wallace (Camp Hill, PA: Foundation Publications, 2011), 61.

64 1 Corinthians 3:2; Hebrews 5:12–13; 1 Peter 2:2.

65 Robert Barclay [1673], *A Catechism and Confession of Faith*, trans. Dean Freiday and Arthur O. Roberts into modern English (Newberg, OR: Barclay Press, 2001), 113.

66 See Ephesians 4:22–24. For examples of people on this path, see John Woolman, *The Journal of John Woolman and a Plea for the Poor* [1774] (Secaucus, NJ: Citadel Press, 1961; Brinton, *Quaker Journals*; Marcelle Martin, *Our Life Is Love: The Quaker Spiritual Journey* (San Francisco: Inner Light Books, 2016).

67 David Johnson, *The Workings of the Spirit of God Within: The Offices of Christ,* Pendle Hill Pamphlet #459 (Wallingford, PA: Pendle Hill Publications, 2019), 22–23.

68 Stirredge, *Strength in Weakness Manifest* [1692], 72–73.

69 Evelyn Sturge, *The Glory of Growing Old* (1950), 7–8, quoted in Britain Yearly Meeting, *Quaker Faith & Practice*, #21.45.

70 Pope Francis, *Laudato Si, On Care for Our Common Home: Encyclical Letter of the Holy Father Francis* (The Vatican: The Catholic Truth Society, 2015), 44–45, 46.

71 Goldsmith, *Practicing the Presence*, 102.

72 Testimony from the National Half-Year's Meeting in Dublin, concerning Abigail Watson, 1753, in *A collection of testimonies concerning several*

ministers of the gospel [1760], 272–73, quoted in Britain Yearly Meeting, *Quaker Faith & Practice*, #21.50.

73 See treatments of the covenant community in Lewis Benson, *Catholic Quakerism* (Philadelphia: Philadelphia Yearly Meeting, 1990), 35–38, and in Douglas Gwyn, *The Call to Radical Faithfulness: Covenant in Quaker Experience* (Philadelphia: Plain Press, 2017), 72–78.

74 See Romans 12:4–8; 1 Corinthians 12:12–31; Ephesians 2:19–22; 1 Peter 2:5.

75 See 1 Corinthians 12:1–11, esp. verse 7.

76 Lewis Benson, *Catholic Quakerism* (Philadelphia: Philadelphia Yearly Meeting, 1968), 38, 40–41. This was later published as *Universal Quakerism*.

77 Fox [1647], *Journal*, ed. Nickalls, 24.

78 Lloyd Lee Wilson, "The Meeting as Covenant Community," in *Essays on the Quaker Vision of the Gospel Order* (Wallingford, PA: Pendle Hill Publications, 1996), 61–72.

79 William Backhouse and James Janson, comps., *A Guide to True Peace or the Excellency of Inward and Spiritual Prayer* [1813] (Wallingford, PA: Pendle Hill, 1979), 2–3, 10–11, 27. This is a compilation of writings by François Fénelon, Jeanne Guyon, and Miguel de Molinos.

Also available from Inner Light Books

William Penn's 'Holy Experiment':
Quaker Truth in Pennsylvania, 1685-1781
By James Proud
> ISBN 978-0-9998332-9-2 (hardcover) $50
> ISBN 978-1-7328239-3-8 (paperback) $35

A Guide to Faithfulness Groups
By Marcelle Martin
> ISBN 978-1-7328239-4-5 (hardcover) $25.00
> ISBN 978-1-7328239-5-2 (paperback) $12.50
> ISBN 978-1-7328239-6-9 (eBook) $10

A Word from the Lost
By David Lewis
> ISBN 978-1-7328239-7-6 (hardcover) $35
> ISBN 978-1-7328239-8-3 (paperback) $25
> ISBN 978-1-7328239-9-0 (eBook) $12.50

In the Stillness
Poems, prayers, reflections
by Elizabeth Mills
> ISBN 978-1-7328239-0-7, (hardcover) $25
> ISBN 978-1-7328239-1-4, (paperback) $12.50
> ISBN 978-1-7328239-2-1, (eBook) $10

Walk Humbly, Serve Boldly
Modern Quakers as Everyday Prophets
by Margery Post Abbott
> ISBN 978-0-9998332-6-1, (hardcover) $45
> ISBN 978-0-9998332-7-8, (paperback) $30
> ISBN 978-0-9998332-8-5, (eBook) $12.50

Primitive Quakerism Revived
by Paul Buckley.

> ISBN 978-0-9998332-2-3 (hardcover) $25
> ISBN 978-0-9998332-3-0 (paperback)$15
> ISBN 978-0-9998332-5-4 (eBook)$10

Primitive Christianity Revived
by William Penn
Translated into Modern English by Paul Buckley

ISBN 978-0-9998332-0-9 (hardcover) $25
ISBN 978-0-9998332-1-6 (paperback) $15
ISBN 978-0-9998332-4-7 (eBook)$10

Jesus, Christ and Servant of God
Meditations on the Gospel According to John
by David Johnson

ISBN 978-0-9970604-6-1 (hardcover) $35
ISBN 978-0-9970604-7-8 (paperback) $25
ISBN 978-0-9970604-8-5 (eBook) $12.50

The Anti-War
by Douglas Gwyn

ISBN 978-0-9970604-3-0, (hardcover)$30
ISBN 978-0-9970604-4-7, (paperback)$17.50
ISBN 978-0-9970604-5-4, (eBook) $10

Our Life Is Love, the Quaker Spiritual Journey
by Marcelle Martin

ISBN 978-0-9970604-0-9, (hardcover)$30
ISBN 978-0-9970604-1-6, (paperback)$17.50
ISBN 978-0-9970604-2-5, (eBook) $10

A Quaker Prayer Life
by David Johnson

ISBN 978-0-9834980-5-6 (hardcover) $20
ISBN 978-0-9834980-6-3 (paperback) $12.50
ISBN 978-0-9834980-7-0 (eBook)) $10

The Essential Elias Hicks
by Paul Buckley

ISBN 978-0-9834980-8-7 (hardcover) $25
ISBN 978-0-9834980-9-4 (paperback) $15
ISBN 978-0-9970604-9-2 (eBook)$10

The Journal of Elias Hicks
edited by Paul Buckley

> ISBN 978-0-9797110-4-6, (hardcover)$50
> ISBN 978-0-9797110-5-3, (paperback)$30

Dear Friend: The Letters and Essays of Elias Hicks
edited by Paul Buckley

> ISBN 978-0-9834980-0-1 (hardcover) $45
> ISBN 978-0-9834980-1-8 (paperback) $25

The Early Quakers and 'the Kingdom of God'
by Gerard Guiton

> ISBN 978-0-9834980-2-5, (hardcover)$45
> ISBN 978-0-9834980-3-2, (paperback)$25
> ISBN 978-0-9834980-4-9, (eBook) $12.50

John Woolman and the Affairs of Truth
edited by James Proud

> ISBN 978-0-9797110-6-0, (hardcover)$45
> ISBN 978-0-9797110-7-7, (paperback)$25

Cousin Ann's Stories for Children by Ann Preston
edited by Richard Beards
illustrated by Stevie French

> ISBN 978-0-9797110-8-4, (hardcover)$20,
> ISBN 978-0-9797110-9-1, (paperback)$12

Counsel to the Christian-Traveller: also Meditations and Experiences
by William Shewen

> ISBN 978-0-9797110-0-8 (hardcover) $25
> ISBN 978-0-9797110-1-5 (paperback) $15

CPSIA information can be obtained
at www.ICGtesting.com
Printed in the USA
LVHW090346130420
652876LV00003BA/8/J

9 781734 630008